Dedicated To:
Saint Thomas Aquinas High School
Overland Park, Kansas

Written By: Abigail Gartland

Hello, my name is St. Thomas Aquinas.

I was born in the year 1225 in Italy!

When I was a young man, I decided to join the Dominicans.

My true passion was to write about the truths of Jesus and share them with the world!

studied so much, and wrote everything that I could!

I wrote and wrote and wrote some more!!

After a few years, the pope asked me to come see him in Rome!

While I was there, I taught students, and created my own schoo

I taught for a long me, and one evening I received a visit from Jesus!

Jesus told me that he was very proud of me for always sharing His teachings and His goodness.

He asked me what I would want for a reward for all of my hard work.

I told Him, that His love was the best reward!

I became a doctor of the church.

I am not like a doctor you would see at a doctor's office. It means I am a teacher of the Church.

Do you want to be more like me?

First, you can start by celebrating with me on my feast day, January 28th!

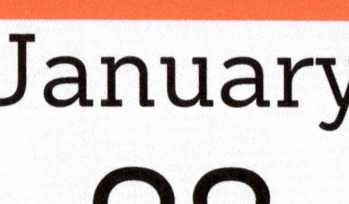

Second, you can read and learn as much as you can. Reading makes you smarter!

You can always count on me to be praying for you for your whole life!

St. Thomas Aquinas
Pray for us!

Copyright:

Clipart: © PentoolPixie © LimeandKiwiDesigns
Licensed purchased: 1/10/2024

About the Author

Abigail Gartland

love the saints and I love my faith. The idea for sharing the stories of the saints with little ones came when my dear friends were expecting their first baby. I wanted to create something as unique and special as our friendship. Each book is dedicated to very special people and groups who have enriched my faith in different ways. I am blessed to write these stories and appreciate the unending support of my family and friends. When I am not writing, I am a middle school teacher. I hope you enjoy these stories. I pray for each and every person who opens one of my books to learn more about the saints.

Abbie

www.ingramcontent.com/pod-product-compliance
Lightning Source LLC
LaVergne TN
LVHW052047070526
838201LV00087B/4905